of

an

Artist

Erika Renee Land

of an Artist

Copyright © 2018 by Erika Renee Land

I thought all this shit up. Well … except the part about my life—you can't make up true life. So, I promise it's just a coincidence if you think something pertains to you.

ISBN 978-1-7322842-0-3

If loving you is wrong, I don't want to be right.
Happy Wife, Happy Life.

Corrissa Land, I love you.

ACKNOWLEDGEMENTS

Thank you, to everyone in San Antonio, TX that helped me grow as a person and writer. You know who you are.

This is how I feel: generalized. Because no one likes to be alone.

ERL

INTRODUCTION

When I started this, I was thinking life isn't always peaches and cream, and not everyone understands the perils of being an artist—including the artist.

So, while this chapbook explores the melancholic states of artistry, know that there are many more sides that are extraordinary and great. My goal is to give some insight into the ups and downs that artists face, and—hopefully—help someone also on their own journey see that they are not alone.

Well, I hope you enjoy it.

1

Kismet

Destiny; Fate.

Do it for the Vine. I'm joking, do it for your soul's delight. And remember, the source of your destiny or how you believe it came into existence is inconsequential to you accepting your purpose.

Kismet is the ultimate Frisbee of life, so aim with intention. Find a way to positively impact as many as you can and stay true to that purpose.

Art brings about an enjoyment that can't be escaped; which is why it's imperative that you figure out your goals early on. This way, when times are hard and you're questioning your purpose, you will have something to fall back on. Because one day, disappointment will find you.

Disappointment is inevitable in that there is no tangible procurement for the emotional impact of an artist's creations, and because you will never be able to gauge the true impact of your work; therefore, sadness may arise.

See, there comes a point in time when you will realize—as every artist does—that your art is not you, that the raw materials you manipulate are not you, and that you are still your sex and color. And, though these attributes should not hinder you, you will have to acknowledge two things:

1.Art cannot change everyone's prejudices against you into admiration for you.

2.No matter how much you create, your dues as an artist will never be paid in full.

The aforementioned facts will be your ultimate struggle, because people will always want something bigger and better.

Nonetheless, you have to keep at it. Kismet says that you will keep at it, because somewhere deep inside you is the need to transcend the bounds of sexism, racism, and bigotry, metaphorically and literally.

2

Depression

Feelings of severe despondency
and dejection.

When we start out as artists there is this flitting, whimsical hope that by expressing ourselves we will bring a little bit of optimism to someone else's life. We hope that someone else will make it another day because our art—in some way—expresses to them, "I exist with you, and just like you I am searching for meaning in this world." However, because you are an artist you strive for more than that satisfaction. You want a way to be remembered after death, and that small difference can lead to dissonance within you.

Possibly, at some point, things will change along your artistic journey and the quandary of feeling misunderstood coupled with the feeling that no one really cares will arise, causing you to examine your motives.

So, when you realize that maybe your art isn't necessarily only about changing the world for the better, but also that you create for other people because you want to be understood, conformity will begin to take over. This will cause you to seek ways to keep the public interested, sometimes by any means necessary.

(Side note: This, by the way, is the true act of selling your soul.)

Subsequently, you will feel the pain of that struggle—between staying true to yourself and doing what's necessary to please others—causing very deep feelings of despondency; enough to depress you.

Becoming an artist is about singularity, but while in search of mass acceptance sometimes it's easier to become what people want you to be. This eventually causes the moments of pure wonder at what initially drove you to become manufactured.

The creation of the faux world that you and those around you created will become too encapsulating. You will then realize that what you first strove for as an artist—acceptance from the world—cannot be enjoyed because you have unwittingly removed yourself from the expanded world.

When I say *world* I mean the expansive anonymous world, as opposed to a bubble built of handlers and bodyguards and lattes in front of cameras.

Deep down we want to change our status from *outsider* to *insider*. We want to use our natural skills to elevate ourselves toward being elite, but in life sometimes our wants backfire and the cycle of depression begins.

As an artist, it is easy to become trapped between who you are and who *they* want you to be. So, you must be careful.

3

Addiction

The fact or condition of being addicted to a particular substance or activity.

We've never been a happy people, thinking that we could bury the past by creating beautiful things, and spreading joy throughout the world by sharing our happy moments on a wide scale. By burying our regrets, sorrows, lost love, and more, in our art we hope that we will be distracted from our own minds. Then we are exposed to our first fan.

Which leads to the amplification of the uneasiness we've always felt about being around unfamiliar people. We ignore our anxieties, however, and fiendishly begin to chase another, and another, and another. And for a short while it works; we become distracted from our own pain, until … fans are no longer enough stimulation. It's at that point that drugs of all kinds can become menacing.

Through fans, we look for validation of who we are until we subsequently fall into living to please them. And, like ash dissipating in the wind, we find our innermost wants and dreams floating away from us. Our ambitions have to take a back seat to the fulfillment of someone else's pleasures.

Habitually, we tend to ignore our anxieties and try to find ways to use our pain to connect to another's pain so that they may find relief. We do this with the hope that in return we will find our own relief, but life doesn't work that way. You have to deal with things head-on.

Two negatives don't always make a positive, and so often we look for other external things to ease our pain. *Or* we run.

Make a mental note of this: *You cannot run away from yourself.*

4

Aloofness

Not friendly or forthcoming;
cool and distant.

Running away from the world you created is frowned upon. No longer wanting the things you wanted is frowned upon. Trying to find a new meaning to life when all your wishes have been granted is often misunderstood, so we search for meaning in places distant from our current situations.

Just as others cannot understand us wanting to be away from the things we previously wanted, artists tend to be just as confused about what is important. The uncertainty lies within the definition of happiness, and no one but you can define it.

As you grow, the source of your creations will change. Unfortunately, people often don't like change and will accuse you of not being authentic. My suggestion is to take on a *Fuck 'em*

mentality. Whoever you are that day is
who you are, and that's the true you.
And now a random poem!

What do you do when you're not broken anymore,
    and that brokenness was your muse?

When you step onto the stage to speak
    and the words no longer come as easy?

When your secret love affair ends
    with the pain hidden deep within?

When you've turned your last bit of pain into a
masterpiece
    that's ready to take the stage for the last time?

When the creative side of you was alive,
    because it thrived on the melancholic side of your
    mind?

What do you do when
    you are free of the sadness that kept you teetering
    with despair?

What do you do when
    the curtain call for the lady that sings the blues
    goes unanswered?

What do you do when
    the brokenness of your soul is no longer your
muse?

You continue to improve and congratulate yourself for walking anew.

5

Paranoia

Unjustified suspicion and mistrust of other people.

Trust is a finicky thing, and the drugs don't help.

It's true that money brings more problems … and more bills, and more people to help guide you, and those that want to hang around you, and those looking to make a buck off of you.

Unfortunately, it's hard to know who has your best interest at heart or who you can trust with your secrets, so always proceed with caution and follow your gut.

Encountering someone with ulterior motives is unavoidable, so you must find a way to minimize your suspicions.

6

Am I an Artist?

There is no validity in self-declaration. See, the double meaning of your life is hinged on how you perceive it and how others receive it. For instance, I've changed and grown on the inside, but other people have not always accepted that change. It's the dichotomy of trying to be your best self and living the way that you think is going to be the most impactful, but others around you build up their own expectations or are unable to let go of your past indiscretions. Which, I suppose, has affected me as an artist; despite what I want the world to know about my art, the fruits of my labor must be justified by someone else. The age-old metaphysical question arises: If I declare something does that make it true?

The sadness of it all is that the people who validated you can abandon you. So, I encourage you to find absolution within yourself and always remember that you are enough.

7

About this Artist!

I like to make the joke that I grew up on Wall Street, which is a true statement—just not the Wall Street that comes to mind when you hear those two words together. I grew up on another Wall Street—in Norfolk, Virginia. In a part of town that was barren of money and prestige. The only thing my Wall Street was known for was being the first street you came to once you crossed the railroad tracks out of the Huntersville neighborhood.

"One of Norfolk's oldest and most intact settlements remaining from the late 19th century, [that] is unique because it was not planned by a company or commission, but developed over time," according to Wikipedia.

The neighborhood that it had turned into by the time I moved to Wall Street, around 1993, was full of indigent people that often raided our house for essentials and flippable items. My sisters and I were in the house during one of the raids, scared shitless as a knock on the front door advanced to a crackhead breaking the sliding glass door on the back of the house, and then rummaging through our belongings.

At 14, I barricaded my sisters and myself in the bathroom and dialed 911, hoping that the strange man would not breach the locked door. Luckily, he didn't, and I am able to relay this story to you. That moment stripped away my ignorance of how dangerous the world is. Before then I'd never realized the fragility between life and death. From that moment until now—and probably until my dying day—this need to save others overwhelms me, which often causes me to struggle with putting myself first. Often, I give too much of myself too soon.

I always thought that I would start my biography off like this: I was born at Sentara Norfolk General on August 9, 1983, fourteen miles due west of the Francis Land House, a National Historic landmark that backdates my family's namesake to the 1630's. On a sprawling 1,020 acres of land, my people cultivated the crops and fields under the mastership of Francis Land and his descendants.

The sad thing is, I don't think a lot of my extended family has been able to progress further past the violence, silence, dejection, and depression of slavery. If it were right for me to place value on another person's happiness, I would say that most of them are stuck in survival mode rather than joyful living. But back to the house.

My experience at the Francis Land house was one of nostalgic heartbreak. I had no expectations of what it would be like walking onto the plantation but was quickly humbled and overwhelmed by the experience. To know that the soil under my feet was plowed by my ancestors, that they had to enter the house through the basement, and that now—in the 21st century—their plight is softened by the tour guide who refers to them as servants, to make the tourists feel comfortable, was heartbreaking. I wanted to scream, "We were fucking slaves, not servants!" But the rational side of me knew that she was only reciting a script written by a politically-correct committee.

But since this is about the nature of some artists—not my biography—I will get back to the last chapter of this book.

8

Joy
A feeling of great pleasure
and happiness.

You may have inferred that my association with art is one of pain, but I assure you that the melancholic conditions of an artist will forever be overshadowed by the triumph that is felt once a project is complete and you have poured your heart and soul into it.

The only way I can describe it is that it's like the feeling a baby has after experiencing ice cream for the first time.

So, remember to keep Nike in mind and "Just do it," be "Off the Wall" like Vans, and embrace yourself like Reebok and scream to the world "I am what I am."

#OfAnArtist
Ask me anything you want on FB.com/erikareneeland or through my website www.ErikaRLand.com

I love you!!!!

of an Artist
Erika Renee Land

Born on August 9th 1983, in Norfolk, Virginia, Erika Renee Land is an American 21st century war poet, known for her numerous essays, fiction novels, various poetry collections, and being a civil rights activist.

She has published two books of poetry. The first was Residual Affects, with fellow veteran KaTisha Smittick that juxtaposes their similar experiences by meshing poetry and photography, and the second book Georgia's Dam, embodies Erika's struggles with Post-traumatic stress disorder, that takes you to the very spots where she created most of her poetry.

Her first fiction series *It's Complicated* highlights the struggles of interpersonal relationships. As a civil rights activist she travels giving the opening speeches for marches, is a member of the NAACP, the National Organization for Women, and the Alliance for Justice to name a few.